Bible Secret Codes

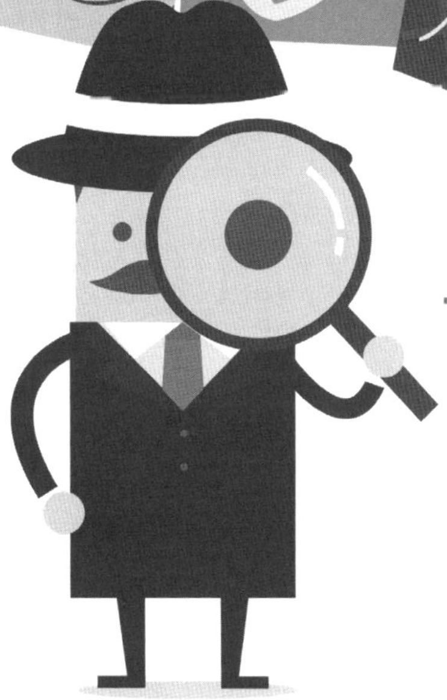

Activity Book

Illustrated by
Michael Denman

3058002100000569

When we read the Bible, we learn what God wants us to do.
We can memorize Bible verses,
so we have God's Word with us all the time!

What does the Bible say? Use the code to find out.

17   15 1 18 9   15 17 7 7 9 2

24 4 16 10   20 4 10 7   17 2   25 24

15 9 1 10 14   14 15 1 14   17

25 17 13 15 14   2 4 14   12 17 2

1 13 1 17 2 12 14   24 4 16.

Psalm 119:11 (NIV)

CODE:

A	B	C	D	E	F	G	H	I	J	K	L	M
1	3	5	7	9	11	13	15	17	19	21	23	25

N	O	P	Q	R	S	T	U	V	W	X	Y	Z
2	4	6	8	10	12	14	16	18	20	22	24	26

God gave Moses the 10 Commandments, or laws,
to teach people the right way to live.

What was the first commandment? Use the code to find out.

___ ___ ___   ___ ___ ___ ___ ___
23 3 15   11 16 2 24 24

___ ___ ___ ___   ___ ___
16 2 17 10   1 3

___ ___ ___ ___ ___   ___ ___ ___ ___
3 13 16 10 9   14 3 8 11

___ ___ ___ ___ ___ ___   ___ ___.
4 10 12 3 9 10   26 10

Exodus 20:3 (NIV)

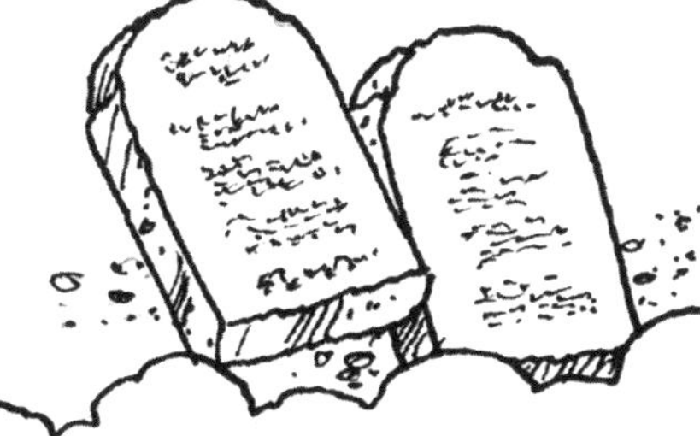

CODE:

A	B	C	D	E	F	G	H	I	J	K	L	M	N	O	P
2	4	6	8	10	12	14	16	18	20	22	24	26	1	3	5

Q	R	S	T	U	V	W	X	Y	Z
7	9	11	13	15	17	19	21	23	25

Jesus gives us the best kind of freedom. When we ask Him to forgive our sins, we have a new life!

What does the Bible say? Use the code to find out.

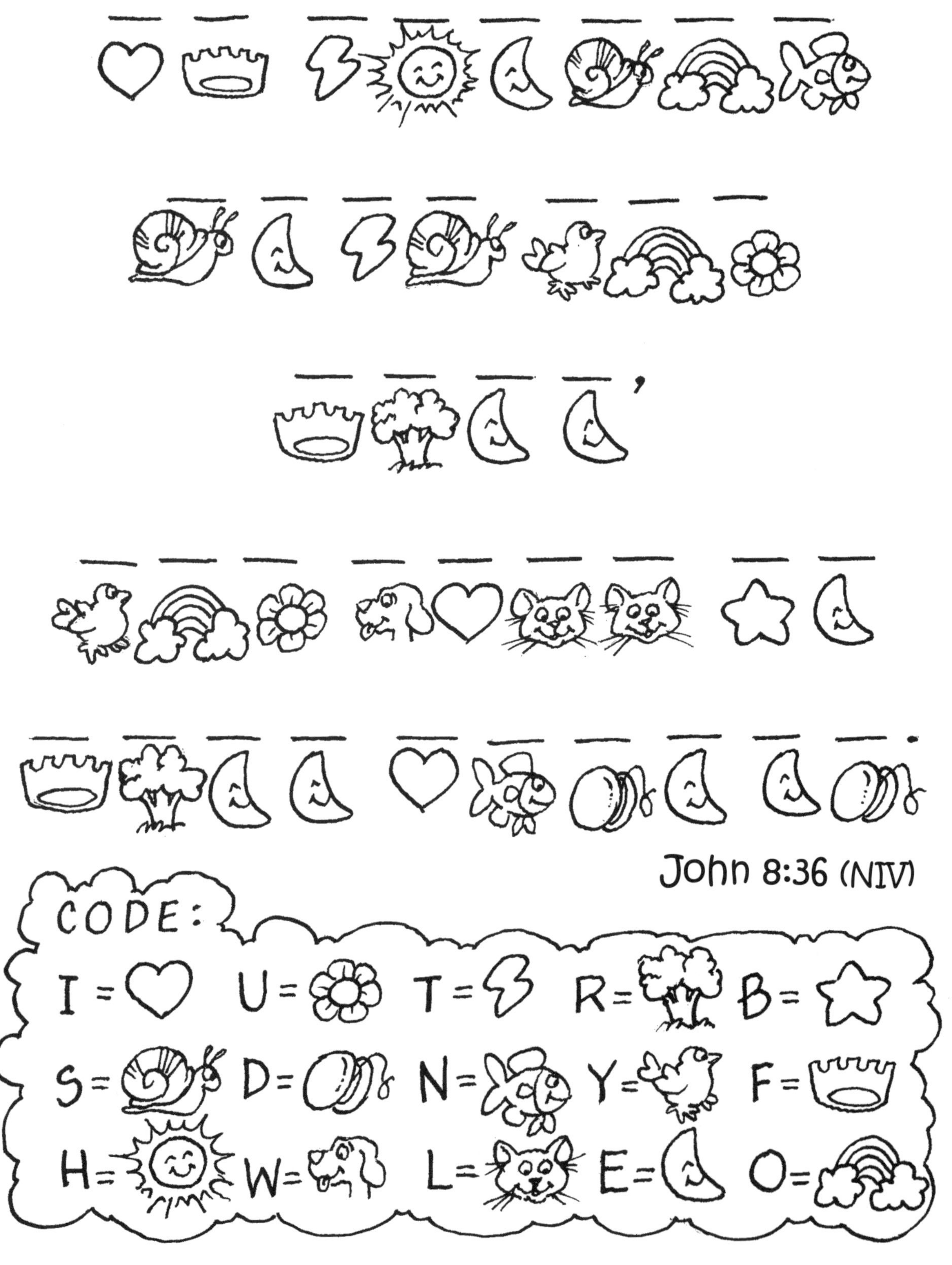

When we help people in need, Jesus is happy with us.

What will He say? Use the code to find out.

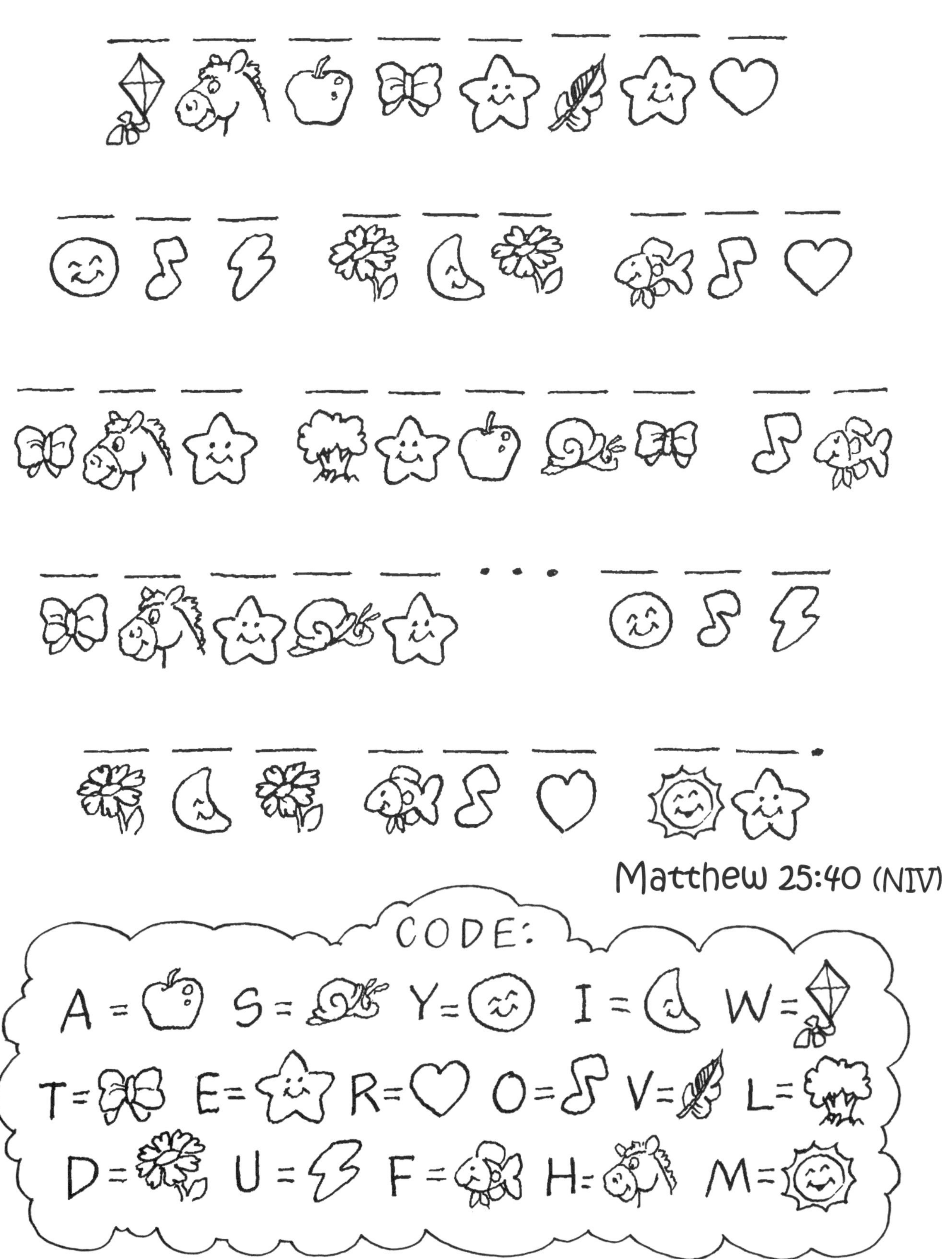

God does so much for us. We should thank Him all the time!

What does the Bible say? Use the code to find out.

In Ephesians 6:10-17, Paul tells us how to stand strong for God by wearing our spiritual armor.

What else does Paul tell us to do? Use the code to find out.

Ephesians 6:18 (NIV)

Young or old, sick or well, God wants us all in His family. We can help people who are hurting and celebrate with people who are happy. We all belong together!

What does the Bible say? Use the code to find out.

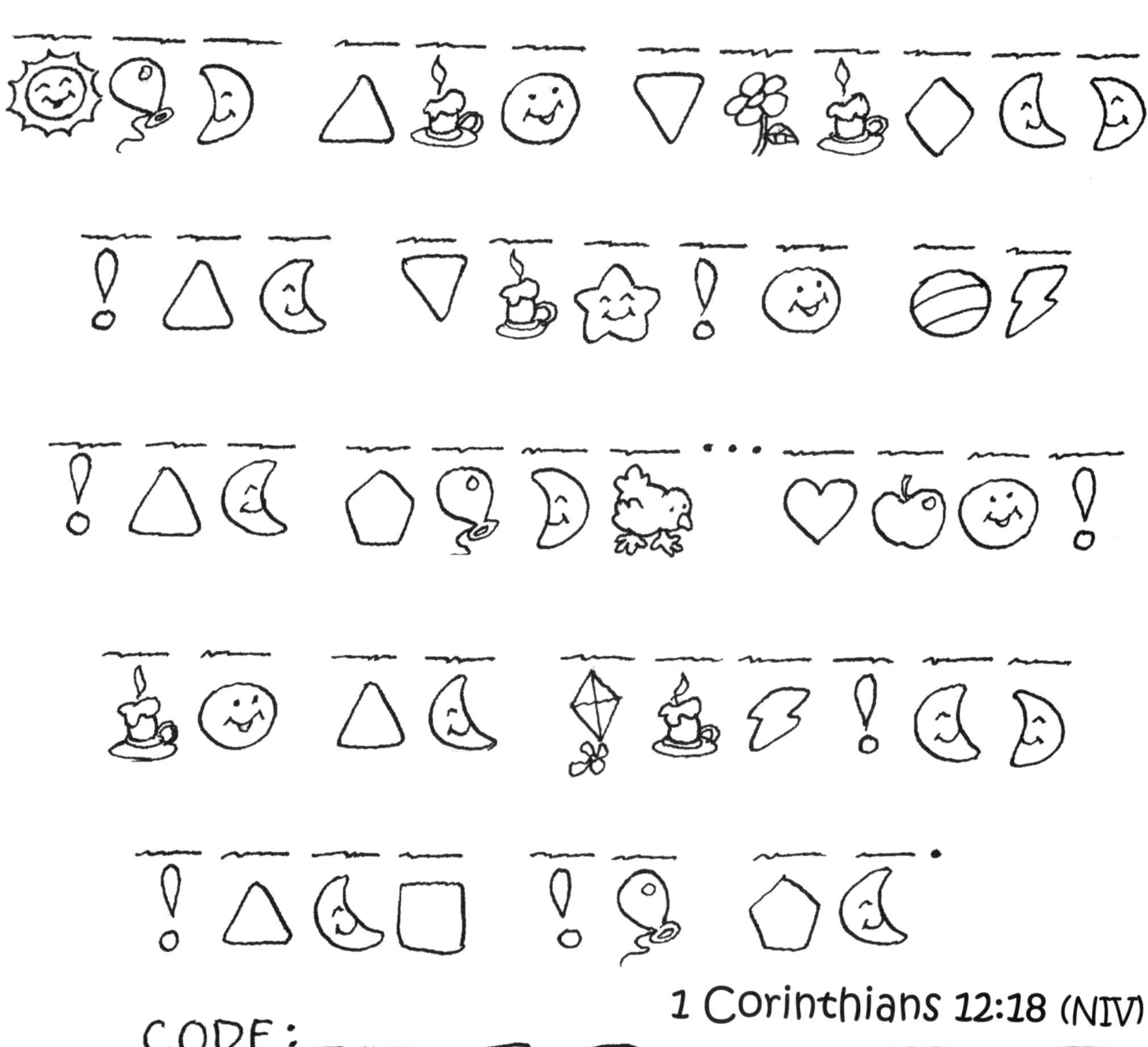

1 Corinthians 12:18 (NIV)

CODE:

J= H= M= S= P= G=

C= R= N= T= E= I= L=

D= B= U= A= O= Y= W=

In the Bible, God chose Joshua to be the new leader of His people. It was a big job, and Joshua was afraid. God told him, "Do not be afraid."

You don't have to be afraid either. Why? Use the code to find out.

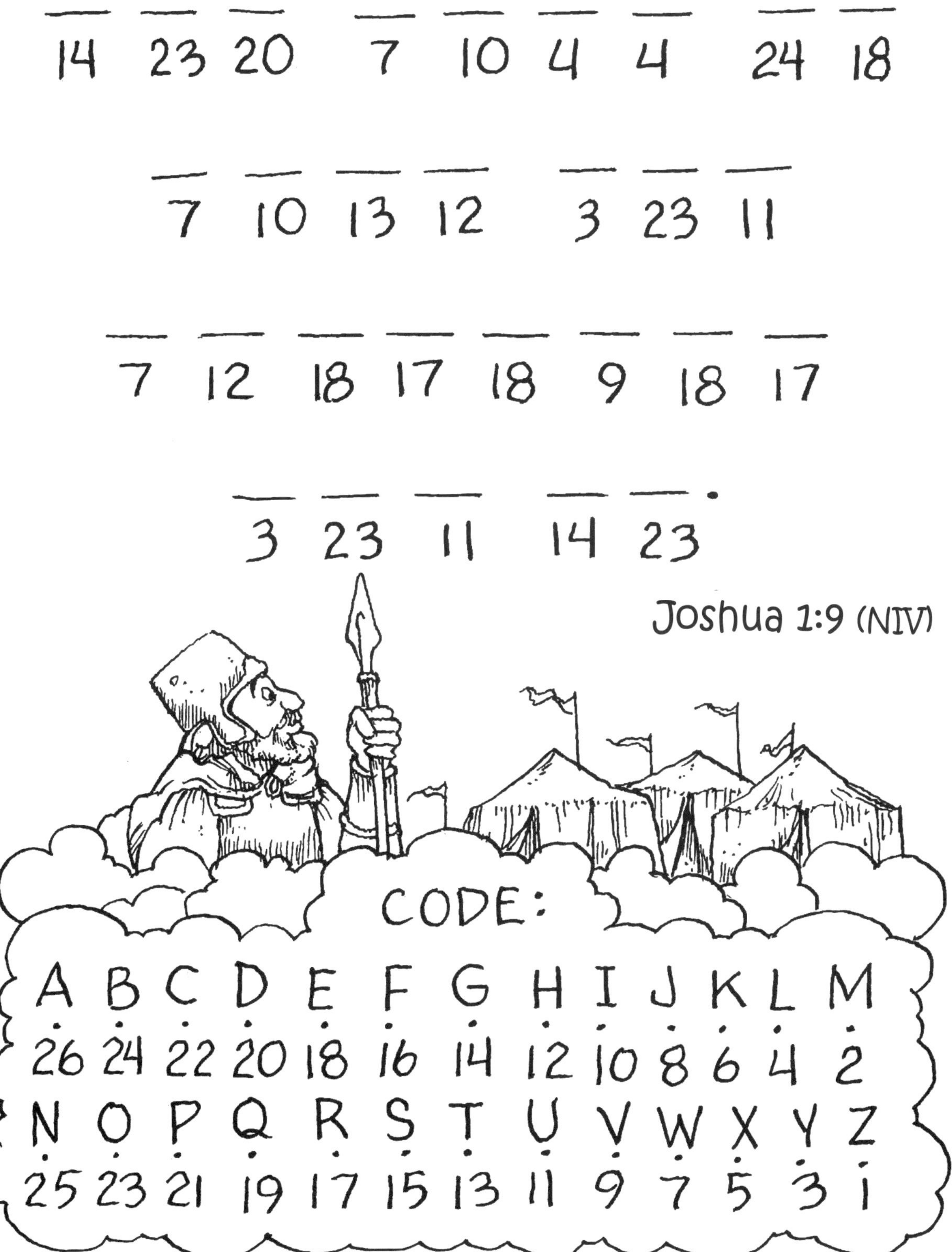

People all around the world worship God.
Our languages may be different. We may sing different songs.
But our love for God and His love for us is the same!

Use the code to read the Bible verse.

___ ___ ___ ___ ___ ___
26 15 15 7 19 22

___ ___ ___ ___ ___ ___ ___ ... ___ ___ ___ ___
13 26 7 18 12 13 8 4 18 15 15

___ ___ ___ ___ ___ ___ ___
24 12 14 22 26 13 23

___ ___ ___ ___ ___ ___ ___ ___ ___ ___ ___ ___ ___
4 12 9 8 19 18 11 25 22 21 12 9 22

___ ___ ___, ___ ___ ___ ___. Psalm 86:9 (NIV)
2 12 6 15 12 9 23

CODE:

Z	Y	X	W	V	U	T	S	R	Q	P	O	N
1	2	3	4	5	6	7	8	9	10	11	12	13
M	L	K	J	I	H	G	F	E	D	C	B	A
14	15	16	17	18	19	20	21	22	23	24	25	26

God wants us to talk to Him all the time.
He loves us!

What does the Bible say? Use the code to find out.

17 2   9 18 9 10 24

12 17 14 16 1 14 17 4 2,

3 24   6 10 1 24 9 10 . . .

6 10 9 12 9 2 14   24 4 16 10

10 9 8 16 9 12 14 12

14 4   13 4 7 .

Philippians 4:6 (NIV)

CODE:

A	B	C	D	E	F	G	H	I	J	K	L	M
1	3	5	7	9	11	13	15	17	19	21	23	25
N	O	P	Q	R	S	T	U	V	W	X	Y	Z
2	4	6	8	10	12	14	16	18	20	22	24	26

Good runners look straight ahead.
Looking back would slow them down or make them trip.

In the Bible, what did Paul say? Use the code to find out.

__   __ __ __ __ __   __ __
10   21 17 18 15 15   23 25

__ __ __ __ __ __   __ __ __
13 23 7 26 17 20   13 12 18

__ __ __ __   __ __   __ __ __
14 23 26 4   13 23   7 10 25

__ __ __   __ __ __ __ __   __ __ __
13 12 18   21 17 10 1 18   16 23 17

__ __ __ __ __   __ __ __
7 12 10 22 12   14 23 20

__ __ __   __ __ __ __ __ __   __ __.
12 26 15   22 26 4 4 18 20   2 18

Philippians 3:14 (NIV)

CODE:

A	B	C	D	E	F	G	H	I	J	K	L	M
26	24	22	20	18	16	14	12	10	8	6	4	2

N	O	P	Q	R	S	T	U	V	W	X	Y	Z
25	23	21	19	17	15	13	11	9	7	5	3	1

Becoming a Christian—a person who lives for Jesus—is easy! The first step is to tell Jesus you have sinned and are sorry.

What does the Bible say? Use the code to find out.

__ __ __   __ __ __ __
26 15 15   19 26 5 22

__ __ __ __ __ __   __ __ __
8 18 13 13 22 23   26 13 23

__ __ __ __   __ __ __ __ __
21 26 15 15   8 19 12 9 7

__ __   __ __ __
12 21   7 19 22

__ __ __ __ __   __ __
20 15 12 9 2   12 21

__ __ __ .
20 12 23   Romans 3:23 (NIV)

CODE:

A	B	C	D	E	F	G	H	I	J	K	L	M
26	25	24	23	22	21	20	19	18	17	16	15	14

N	O	P	Q	R	S	T	U	V	W	X	Y	Z
13	12	11	10	9	8	7	6	5	4	3	2	1

God has a different way of looking at people.
God doesn't just see the outside; He sees the inside too.
What is on the inside matters most to Him.

What does the Bible say? Use the code to find out.

___ ___ ___ ___ ___ ___   ___ ___ ___ ___   ___ ___
11 22 12 11 15 22   15 12 12 16   26 7

___ ___ ___   ___ ___ ___ ___ ___ ___ ___
7 19 22   12 6 7 4 26 9 23

___ ___ ___ ___ ___ ___ ___ ___ ___ ___,   ___ ___ ___
26 11 11 22 26 9 26 13 24 22,   25 6 7

___ ___ ___   ___ ___ ___ ___   ___ ___ ___ ___ ___
7 19 22   15 12 9 23   15 12 12 16 8

___ ___   ___ ___ ___   ___ ___ ___ ___ ___.
26 7   7 19 22   19 22 26 9 7.

1 Samuel 16:7 (NIV)

CODE:

Z	Y	X	W	V	U	T	S	R	Q	P	O	N
1	2	3	4	5	6	7	8	9	10	11	12	13
M	**L**	**K**	**J**	**I**	**H**	**G**	**F**	**E**	**D**	**C**	**B**	**A**
14	15	16	17	18	19	20	21	22	23	24	25	26

When we don't know what to do, we can ask God!
He will help us solve the problem, answer the question,
or find the right path.

What does the Bible say? Use the code to find out.

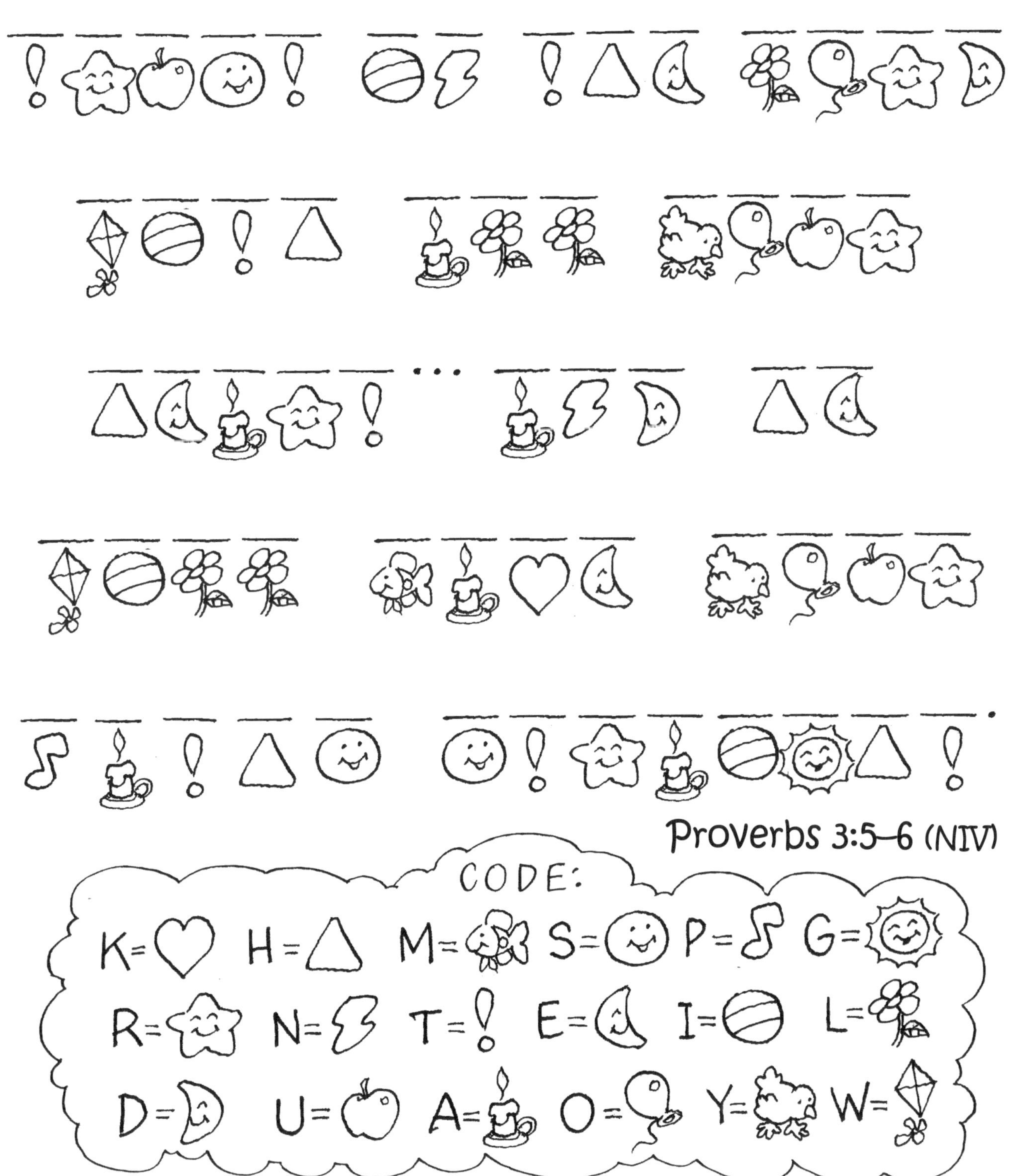

God is watching over you all the time.
He cares so much for you!

What does the Bible say? Use the code to find out.

Psalm 91:11 (NIV)

CODE:

S= H= O= R= E= W=
M= I= G= L= C= A=
N= D= T= U= Y=